The Forensics of Freedom

Karey Thomas

© KT Empowers, LLC

www.ktempowers.com

All rights reserved. No part of this publication may be reproduced, distributed, or transmitted in any form or by any means, including photocopying, recording, or other electronic or mechanical methods, without the prior written permission of the publisher, except in the case of brief quotations embodied in critical reviews and certain other noncommercial uses permitted by copyright law.

Scripture quotations identified as "ESV" are from The ESV® Bible (The Holy Bible, English Standard Version®). ESV® Text Edition: 2016. Copyright © 2001 by Crossway, a publishing ministry of Good News Publishers.

Scripture quotations identified as "GW" are from GOD'S WORD®, © 1995 God's Word to the Nations. Used by permission of God's Word Mission Society.

Scripture quotations identified as "KJV" are from the King James Version of the Bible.

Scripture quotations identified as "NIV" are from THE HOLY BIBLE, NEW INTERNATIONAL VERSION®, NIV® Copyright © 1973, 1978, 1984, 2011 by Biblica, Inc.® Used by permission. All rights reserved worldwide.

Editor: PurposeMasters - www.purposemasters.com

ISBN: 9798653592133

Dedication

To My Wife, Sharonda- Thank you for believing in me, loving me, and pushing me. Your love has transformed me from the inside-out. Your tenacity has been the driving force behind my success. You are the one who floats my boat and finds my lost remote.

To My Family, Local and Global, Natural and Spiritual- I love you all.

To My Spiritual Father, Supreme Archbishop Emmanuel OjoPowerson- The Man of God who embraced me in the Grace. I thank God for your life. Words cannot express the profound impact of the time spent in impartation and activation. I honor the man and the mantle.

Above all, this book is dedicated to the Lord Jesus Christ. All that I am and will ever be is because Jesus is Lord.

Table of Contents

Foreword

Introduction

Tracing Truth..1

Freedom in HD...7

The Paradox of Peace....................................13

The Peninsula of Peace.................................23

Spiritual Check-Up..27

BLOOD Pressure..35

The Source of Bondage.................................39

Forensic Proofs...45

Our Victory...69

Foreword

Several years ago, while attempting to ameliorate poverty in the inner-city of Houston, Texas, I had the opportunity to meet Karey Thomas. As he shared his story, I came to realize poor choices demanded a loss of freedom for Karey Thomas. Years later, Karey is moving on. He, his wife Sharonda, and their children are a lovely family. A sense of loss from what could have been a very different "life lived" moves them to want to "catch up". Karey's life is not back to "normal", but rather "supernormal". He is like a zooming plane jetting across the sky to its next destination.

Karey's new-found freedom was certainly civil freedom, but also a freedom found in the open arms of God. This freedom to be with family and God propelled him in ways that were unimaginable. First, he wanted to tell others about this God who had freed his soul. The Thomas's started a home church and reached out to others whose freedom had been restored. Groups within the church were then organized to visit both men's and women's prisons to encourage them to reach for freedom and to know God. I was amazed at their high energy level.

Secondly, Karey's dreams were big and full of possibility. For instance, recidivism is rampant because those recently released to freedom cannot find jobs and end up being reincarcerated. One idea was to form companies owned by these newcomers to freedom so they and others would be able to sustain themselves.

Aside from his energy for life, Karey has a deep intellect (I had to read the book twice to understand it!). As you read "The Forensics of Freedom", be prepared to meet a very loving God waiting for you.

Jerry McIntosh
Co-Founder of Administaff, Business Pioneer, and Philanthropist

Introduction

This book was birthed out of disappointment. I was initially going to teach this message locally, but a convergence of situations caused it to be halted. I felt burdened and robbed, unaware that God's divine plan was already in motion for something greater than I could ever imagine. I knew the message still needed to be taught, so I took it to a place where people needed it the most…the prisons.

As I began to teach, something unique started to take place. Testimonies poured in of people experiencing supernatural deliverance and breakthrough. I was moved to begin to pray for people individually, both those I knew and those I didn't know. A person with 99 YEARS was granted parole. A person with a LIFE sentence was set free. A person with a PENDING case was let go. It was then that an anointing was discovered.

A piercing thought resonated within, *"surely bondage is beyond 4 walls"*. I now travel worldwide with this message and have the opportunity to watch people be liberated from all types of bondages: emotional, financial, physical, relational, social, cultural, etc. This ultimately led to the desire to encapsulate this teaching in written form to reach far beyond the limitations of time. Through this book, I desire for all people to obtain the true meaning of what free indeed actually is.

1

Tracing Truth

The conspiracy of animal-human evolution is a false theory! Man is the only species in creation that shares God's image and likeness. Animals operate on instinct and nature. Now is it that humans don't have instincts? Of course, we do! Nevertheless, we also have intellect and reasoning to come to a logical conclusion of a matter. *For as a man thinketh in his heart, so is he (Proverbs 23:7).* The ability to think, in and of itself, gives us mastery over the default and innately channels our dominion over all creation.

Furthermore, the rest of creation dominates by its God-given design and nature. For example: A lion doesn't think its way out of a territory. He shows up and says, "IT'S

MINE because I'm here!" Without dialect the Indian Ocean says, "Don't get too close trying to find those lost planes or else I'll swallow you too!"

Though our ability to rationalize gives us the superiority in the earth, that doesn't mean we lack similarity with other creatures. There's a nature within us all that can only be described to the likes of an animal because of the ferociousness it carries! Furthermore, we are creatures of multiple facets which gives us a different dynamic to the Grace of Life.

We're CREATURES OF EMOTIONS: We possess the ability to feel internally and sympathize. Depending on how connected we are with another, it awakens a capacity to travail in compounded burdens or rejoice in collateral joy.

We're CREATURES OF PRODUCTION: We are human "beings" not human "doings". BEINGS produce and reproduce. When God formed man from the dust of the Earth, He breathed into him the breath of life. Purposefully, He called him ADAM which means DUST. Dust is ENOS ("man" in Hebrew); enos means BLOOD; blood means COVENANT; where there's covenant there's a TRANSACTION; a successful transaction is a DEAL; a deal means BUSINESS; and business means PRODUCTION!

We're CREATURES OF VISUAL ACCOMMODATION: This is based on the ability to change our focus based on what we see and whether we want/don't want to see a thing. We're by nature categorized as predators along with eagles, wolves, and snakes. This is because we have binocular vision. Notice, most predatory animals have their two eyes positioned to the front of their face. A lot of animals considered "prey" have eyes on the side of their head, making it more difficult to key in on one thing.

We're CREATURES OF PROCESS: We must go through instances physically, mentally, and spiritually in order to truly understand.

We're CREATURES OF HABIT: According to Computer Scientist and Serial Entrepreneur, Alex Pentland, "We humans suffer from an advanced case of self-delusion. We like to see ourselves as free-willed, conscious beings, self-governing, and set apart from other animals by our capacity for reasoning". Note this: "Even though familiarity breeds contempt, it also breeds endorphins."

We're CREATURES OF HABITAT in specifics and in terms of biology, but CREATURES OF HABITATION when it comes to any state of dwelling. I mean ANY! We can even dwell on a situation mentally and that's what we will conform to. Now this creature of habitation part is most vital as you will see throughout this entire book. "Conformity" is the trace of evidence as to why we find ourselves where we find ourselves.

Adapting is inevitable. No matter where you drop us,

in a fortunate place or unfortunate place, once a part of us accepts it, WE WILL ADJUST. I used to think that while taking a bath, once my hands and feet became wrinkle that meant "it was time to get out" because I've been in the tub too long. Well I later learned that just wasn't true. Did you know that? Our faculties wrinkle because it's adjusting to grip the water that it's submerged in. The point being made is even without being told our bodies naturally embrace their surroundings.

So, what if you're surrounded by or submerged in bondage? I believe that this makes the case for recidivism. Because if "bondage" in any area has become one's own norm then freedom from that bondage is subconsciously abnormal. Therefore, no matter how much of life apart from that bondage is presented, without a renewed mind it'll always be foreign to the hearer. So now this identifies a peculiar yet all so common problem that's often overlooked. The problem is not doing the bondage now…the problem is "doing free" from the bondage! You've been beaten up for so long that you have mistaken love for being punched. If he or she is not knocking you to the ground or verbally abusing you, then you don't believe that you're actually being loved…BONDAGE! Your

> *"The problem is not doing bondage now, the problem is 'doing free' from the bondage"*

self-esteem has been so low for so long that you disqualify yourself from even applying for a higher position in life…BONDAGE! Poverty has been your portion for generations, so every nice gesture offered, or opportunity presented you is counted as suspicious and somebody trying to take advantage of you…BONDAGE! Offended at life BONDAGE! Blaming others…BONDAGE! Perpetual victim syndrome…BONDAGE!

I believe that the heart of any bondage cannot be identified on the surface, rather it must be traced. Judging matters, and superficial conditions will more than likely lead to a path away from the actual issue than towards it. The reason for this is natural. We have the propensity of becoming curiously anxious while in the dark of uncertainty. In the school of Deep-Sea Diving, the divers know this all too well. While exploring caves beneath the ocean there are "black holes" that are very dangerous. These "black holes" are recommended to be avoided. Reason being, once you're engulfed in darkness it's impossible to decipher which way is up. Under those circumstances, we panic and begin to compare every condition (we bump into) to that which is commonplace. In consequence, we forfeit all the dynamics of convictions that are to be earned through research and patience. We prematurely come to a reasonable conclusion, never reaching the root to bring it to the surface.

The rationale becomes so bias because emotions only

gravitate towards that which is superficial. Why? Because at least that which is superficial can be seen and what's in sight is the only thing that appears to be relevant.

TRUTH IS TRACED AND LEADS A TRAIL

The excavation of a matter will undoubtedly unearth factors and fossils that could never be reached without breaking the fallow ground. The more you dig and examine, the more you'll find. Notice, merely digging is not enough. The same is so for "human conditions". One must be willing to go beyond the surface of pain and pride to reveal the unreachable truth. An investigation must be launched! All evidence must be put on the table for careful consideration and practical scrutiny.

As we explore hidden areas of your life, expect to experience adverse energy coming to the surface. This will highlight what may be the need for deliverance in certain unknown areas.

Here lies the study of the flesh. The perusal of the soul. The appraisal of the spirit. The analysis of liberty in order to compare and contrast. This is "The Forensics of Freedom!"

2

Freedom In HD

As a child I remember waking up on Saturday mornings to watch Kung-Fu. My favorite person to watch was none other than the G.O.A.T. himself, Mr. Bruce Lee. Those old martial arts movies had their own dynamic of delayed response. You would see their lips moving, but the words wouldn't be spoken until 5 seconds later. Initially, I thought it was the translation, then I noticed that it would do the same thing with a punch and a kick! This phenomenon just about ruined the anticipation in the movie.

Later in life I recognized this exact same effect when I bought "bootleg" DVDs. Ironically, it was quite the opposite. I would hear the sounds first, then 5-10 seconds later see the action. In both cases I'd rather mute the TV and turn the closed captioning on! Why? Because, THE AUDIO DIDN'T MATCH THE VIDEO! Whew! Upon comparison, I realized that one of the movies is foreign and the other is just not authentic, but in both the audio/video synchronicity was off.

Likewise, it is so with FREEDOM. Somehow, we've redefined it and watered it down to make it seem more accessible to everyone. This compromise has deceived mankind to believe that ALL freedom is by default and not a byproduct of choice. So now masses of individuals walk around with a foreign freedom that just doesn't look like freedom, or a questionable freedom that is not authentic! Let me introduce you to Freedom in High Definition!

'Freedom' is a 2-syllable word that really consist through etymology terms of two words. 'FREE' & 'DOM'! 'Free' as an adjective means not under the control or in the power of another. This also implies the ability to do or act as one wishes. "Dom" perhaps means 'domein' which is an old French word that means 'belonging to a lord'. The sub secondary meaning is "an area of territory owned or controlled by a ruler or government". However, the latter would totally contradict the primary root words for "freedom". The earlier mentioned

"Freedom IS What Freedom DOES..."

'domein' leads us to the Middle English word 'domain'. This word 'domain' is a field of action, thought, influence, persuasion, preference, etc. So, for example, a 'kingdom' is the territory of the KING'S DOMAIN. The movements (action) are dictated by the king. Nothing is done without the king in mind (thoughts). Everything supports the king's ideas and gives him the advantage (influence & persuasion). On top of that, operations are functioning and executed to the king's liking and favor (preference). Now above all, let this be noted: There is no kingdom without there first being a king! Likewise, there is no freedom without a dominating precedence of FREE!

The domain of FREE (freedom) is the territory dominated in a field of action, thought, influence, persuasion, preference of being free. If this was stocks and business, 'free' would be the majority shareholder; therefore "owning" the company. The Bible says we get this advantage by investing in its truth. John 8:32 says…"*and you will know the truth and the truth will MAKE you free.*" There's a difference between being MADE free and being SET free. Many are 'set free' without being 'made free'. When an individual is 'set free' without being 'made free' that person is at liberty to continue to be who they've always been. This will always lead back to bondage because being 'set free' without being 'made free' only extends the jurisdiction of bondage.

Being 'made free' is when a dynamic transformation takes place. When you're 'made free' you carry the grace of liberty that cannot be distracted by unfortunate dictates.

Therefore, the word 'make' in the text can only be used interchangeably with the word "set" if it takes on the implication of or likened to -SETting- a clock or being -set- for life financially. Meaning, TRUTH has the ability to radically change you and endow you into a new form of being. John 8:36 concurs with *verse 32* by letting us know that true freedom is a thing we don't just describe.

v.36 Therefore if the Son makes you free, you <u>will be</u> free indeed.

"Will be" speaks of volition. You must want to be free and be a volunteer in freedom's camp.

"...free INDEED"

"Indeed" is a higher level of certainty. In Luke 24 with much doubt concerning Jesus' resurrection, the eleven disciples were told, *"The Lord is risen 'indeed', and has appeared to Simon."* They didn't say, "He has risen , now go check the scriptures". No! "Indeed" means something has taken place that has been witnessed! It was made apparent to some...ie. Not just in theory! He really was gone from the tomb. Angels really spoke to the women (Matthew 28:5). He really appeared to Simon (John 8:34). He really comforted Mary Magdalene (John 20:11-18).

"Indeed" insinuated action being manifested. So, 'indeed' goes beyond being a "faith confession". Many people only "speak to believe" but Paul says, "we believe therefore we speak" (2 Corinthians 4:13). Now since "faith without works is dead" (James 2:26), whatever we truly believe we put action to it consciously and subconsciously. The point being made is this: When you're truly "free indeed" it won't be a mystery. Because when you're truly "free indeed" there's always some type of "deed" that you're "in" to validate your freedom!

Question: Doesn't the Bible say, "Oh taste and see that the Lord is good (Psalm 34:8)?" According to Matthew 5. Are you the LIGHT of the world? Are you the SALT of the EARTH? Well 'salt' is for taste and 'light' is to see. The reason that others aren't tasting and seeing that the Lord is good is because you're not shining and giving them any flavor!

> *When the Lord turned again the captivity of Zion, WE WERE LIKE THEM THAT DREAM. Then was our mouth filled with laughter, and our tongues with singing: THEN SAID THEY AMONG THE HEATHEN, THE LORD HAS DONE GREAT THINGS FOR THEM. The Lord has done great things for us; whereof we are glad.* **Turn again our captivity**, *O Lord, as the streams in the south.*
> PSALM 126:1-4 (KJV)

I'm about to make a strong statement to give you a REALITY CHECK of REVELATION: Any part of your life that doesn't look like a dream or cause others that are captive to dream IS A BONDAGE!

3

The Paradox of Peace

Freedom is one of the few things in life that you can converse about without bringing up the other side of the spectrum. However, it would be a total injustice to not point out what freedom "isn't" and could be mistaken to be. So, let's talk a little bit about bondage.

"And when Gideon perceived that he was an angel of the Lord, Gideon said, Alas, O Lord God! for because I have seen an angel of the Lord face to face.
23And the Lord said unto him, Peace be unto thee; fear not: thou shalt not die.
24Then Gideon built an altar there unto the Lord, and called it Jehovah–shalom: unto this day it is yet in Ophrah of the Abi–ezrites.

25 And it came to pass the same night, that the Lord said unto him, Take thy father's young bullock, even the second bullock of seven years old, and throw down the altar of Baal that thy father hath, and cut down the grove that is by it:
26 And build an altar unto the Lord thy God upon the top of this rock, in the ordered place, and take the second bullock, and offer a burnt sacrifice with the wood of the grove which thou shalt cut down.
27 Then Gideon took ten men of his servants, and did as the Lord had said unto him: and so it was, because he feared his father's household, and the men of the city, that he could not do it by day, that he did it by night."
JUDGES 6:22-27 (KJV)

There are 4 general paramount interests that come to mind when we hear the name Gideon.

1) The Fleece (Judges 6:36-40)
2) The 300 Men Army (Judges 7)
3) The Altar called Jehovah-Shalom (Judges 6:24)
4) Free Bibles (not okay to steal from the motel)

The "Jehovah-Shalom" has taken precedence over all others throughout the years. Most don't even know that it was an altar. It's become almost cliché due to its popularity in mostly all religious facets. Now I want us to identify that the construct of this altar was based on bondages. Let's dissect the scenario surrounding the altar being built.

"And the children of Israel did evil in the sight of the Lord: and the Lord delivered them into the hand of Midian seven years.
2And the hand of Midian prevailed against Israel: and because of the Midianites the children of Israel made them the dens which are in the mountains, and caves, and strong holds.
3And so it was, when Israel had sown, that the Midianites came up, and the Amalekites, and the children of the east, even they came up against them;
4And they encamped against them, and destroyed the increase of the earth, till thou come unto Gaza, and left no sustenance for Israel, neither sheep, nor ox, nor ass.
5For they came up with their cattle and their tents, and they came as grasshoppers for multitude; for both they and their camels were without number: and they entered into the land to destroy it.
6And Israel was greatly impoverished because of the Midianites; and the children of Israel cried unto the Lord.
7And it came to pass, when the children of Israel cried unto the Lord because of the Midianites,
8That the Lord sent a prophet unto the children of Israel, which said unto them, Thus saith the Lord God of Israel, I brought you up from Egypt, and brought you forth out of the house of bondage;
9And I delivered you out of the hand of the Egyptians, and out of the hand of all that oppressed you, and drave them out from before you, and gave you their land;
10And I said unto you, I am the Lord your God; fear not the

gods of the Amorites, in whose land ye dwell: but ye have not obeyed my voice."
JUDGES 6:1-10 (KJV)

In verses 1-2 the children of Israel have a consistent track of doing evil and rebelling against THE LORD, but notice the evil wasn't against others. If you're constantly propelled (not compelled) to do things contrary to God's purpose for your life, there's a need to cry out now and seek deliverance from the bondage of *"wicked propulsion"!*

In Verses 3-6, every time Israel would sow, the enemy opposed them until they were poor and deprived of strength and vitality. I you notice constant adversity during your time of planting (not harvest!) and/or your seeds diminishing in size, it's purpose is to bring irritation and despair. You should pray and seek deliverance from the bondage of the *"locust & caterpillar"!*

Next, in verses 7-10 the children of Israel cried unto the Lord; and they got God's attention. However, crying doesn't always get you loosed. You'll only feel better. For them, because of the callousness of their heart, "crying" was the only sign of them being humble. So, the Lord had compassion, **but He did not** lend His ear to them. Instead, He sent them a prophet to inform them of their neglect. This was His way of giving them the "forensics of their bondage!"

You can't put your faith in crying. Furthermore, if

you're crying more than commanding and decreeing, it's an indication of a bondage. Their ears were desensitized to the voice of the Lord God. Therefore, their voice had become mute in the spirit realm. To break this type of bondage you should pray:

"Lord, give me a reigning ear to hear Your voice above any other voice AND Wherever my voice is silent in the place of supposed to be being heard- BLOOD OF JESUS speak for me! In Jesus' Name, AMEN!"

"And there came an angel of the Lord, and sat under an oak which was in Ophrah, that pertained unto Joash the Abi–ezrite: and his son Gideon threshed wheat by the winepress, to hide it from the Midianites.

12 And the angel of the Lord appeared unto him, and said unto him, The Lord is with thee, thou mighty man of valour.

13 And Gideon said unto him, Oh my Lord, if the Lord be with us, why then is all this befallen us? and where be all his miracles which our fathers told us of, saying, Did not the Lord bring us up from Egypt? but now the Lord hath forsaken us, and delivered us into the hands of the Midianites.

14 And the Lord looked upon him, and said, Go in this thy might, and thou shalt save Israel from the hand of the Midianites: have not I sent thee?

15 And he said unto him, Oh my Lord, wherewith shall I save Israel? behold, my family is poor in Manasseh, and I am the least in my father's house.

16And the Lord said unto him, Surely I will be with thee, and thou shalt smite the Midianites as one man.
17And he said unto him, If now I have found grace in thy sight, then shew me a sign that thou talkest with me.
18Depart not hence, I pray thee, until I come unto thee, and bring forth my present, and set it before thee. And he said, I will tarry until thou come again.
19And Gideon went in, and made ready a kid, and unleavened cakes of an ephah of flour: the flesh he put in a basket, and he put the broth in a pot, and brought it out unto him under the oak, and presented it.
20And the angel of God said unto him, Take the flesh and the unleavened cakes, and lay them upon this rock, and pour out the broth. And he did so.
21Then the angel of the Lord put forth the end of the staff that was in his hand, and touched the flesh and the unleavened cakes; and there rose up fire out of the rock, and consumed the flesh and the unleavened cakes. Then the angel of the Lord departed out of his sight."
JUDGES 6:11-21 (KJV)

In verses 11-12, the angel of the Lord found Gideon hiding yet called him "a mighty man of valor". Though most men's groups have adopted this salutation, it was contrary to his current disposition (of hiding) and contradictory to the embargo attached to his name. Contrary to popular belief, Gideon doesn't mean mighty man of valor. That's why he wasn't addressed by his name. Gideon means 'destroyer' and has a co-meaning of 'one who has a STUMP in place of a hand'. WOW! <u>If your efforts are STUMPED, you can't receive your blessings!</u>

And finally, in verses 13-21, Gideon was called a mighty man of valor. Why and How? Simply because *"the Lord was with him".* Nevertheless, Gideon questioned, "If the Lord is with me, why has all of these things befallen my people?" He was in a circumstantial bondage of adverse uncertainty which brought about adverse bondage in circumstantial uncertainty. Some of us don't doubt that God's omnipresence is "with" us. We're just unsure if God is "for" us right now! If you need encouragement and assurance here's your prayer:

(Psalm 86:17) Lord show me a token for good; that they which hate me may see it, and be ashamed because You, Lord, have helped me & comforted me- In Jesus' Name.

Now we've reached our foundational text, which is amid iniquitous bondage. This was brought in by the children of Israel themselves and those before them. Gideon was now convinced! Since the Lord said to him, "Peace be unto thee", Gideon built the altar "Jehovah-Shalom" which means "The Lord is Peace".

One would think that that should conclude the story: The Lord spoke, peace was declared, the altar was built, and peace was established…THE END! However, we see that what looked to be the end of a dilemma, really was a transitional point for deliverance through obedience. If I could narrate a paraphrase without changing the narrative, I would imagine the Lord addressing Gideon this way: "You call Me "Peace" now here's what "Peace" is instructing you to do in order to be intimate with Me... Go get a specific offering and THROW DOWN the "high places" that your family and friends love to worship/party at!" (verse 25).

THROW DOWN. How does "throwing" something "down" exhibit peace? Many lack the proper perspective of peace and only settle for a convenient aspect suitable for their comfortability. Matthew 5:9 says, "Blessed are the PEACEMAKERS." Somehow we've substituted "peacemakers" with "pacifiers". Listen, peace at any cost is not peace at all! Sometimes in order to "make peace" you must go to war with the prohibitor of that peace. This was a serious test of obedience for Gideon that required courage and heart. That's why verse 27 tells us that *he couldn't do it by day, so he did it at night.* Had he gotten caught throwing down that Altar of Baal- they would've killed him...in his mind.

"Peace at any cost is not peace at all!"

After destroying the Altar of Baal, the Lord told him to BUILD another altar and SACRIFICE (verse 26)! So why was there so much required after constructing the first altar? The reason is because it was an altar built for 'mere' peace, but he named it 'Shalom'.

God didn't grant Gideon mere peace. He told him in verse 23:

    A. "Peace be unto you"
    B. "Fear not"
    C. "You shall not die"

God granted him wholeness, but Gideon was settling for a temporal sense of peace. Moreover, the instructions to THROW DOWN and BUILD are prophetic instructions to bring clearance and stability in our lives. We 'throw down' every hindrance that threatens our security of righteousness. We 'build' a parameter of testimonies and think on those things when disturbances of life present themselves.

Peace is a bi product of our salvation. No matter what's going on or not going on, we should still sense a peace within. We have the peace of God, the peace in God, and the peace with God! Mere peace is for bondage-shalom is for freedom!

- ❖ You can dictate "peace"; shalom is a mutual agreement
- ❖ Peace can be partial; shalom is whole
- ❖ One can call a truce (peace treaty); shalom is the condition of peace
- ❖ Peace is a temporary pact; shalom is a permanent agreement

- Peace can be negative, the absence of commotion; Shalom is positive, the presence of serenity
- Peace is alright in coping with "a void"; Shalom is completeness despite an apparent lack!

Shalom in its essence means nothing missing, nothing broken. Don't overlook, settle, or underestimate the barriers to possessing peace (shalom). The problem are those things that we allow to remain that are assigned to disturb or keeps us from keeping that peace! If you're going to have the right perspective of peace; you're gonna have to tear down places of idolatry in your life that exist now- even if they pre-date you!

4

The PENINSULA of Peace

Story time:

The fishermen were miles out on the deep doing what they do best, despite of what seemed to be common conditions for the current season. Storms regularly hit eastern and southeastern India within two-thirds of the latter months yearly. Many warnings were given with lackadaisical effort before the storm, but all were disregarded as exaggeration due to cultural familiarity. With great arrogance and confidence that, "this too shall pass, just as many others have", the anglers continued their quest for sport.

The conditions escalated at a pace more rapid than it often did before. This is the time that most journeymen decide to call it a day and head in to shore. In the process of doing so, the ecstatic advisory came over the radio. The fishermen became stone faced as they realized by now it was too late. This wasn't an ordinary thunderstorm to be weathered. What approached this coast, brewing in the midst of the Indian Ocean, was a cyclone!

Panic struck by land and by sea. Navigating through the boisterous adversity, the marine operator placed ship-to-shore calls. The lines were tied up and communication crossed due to the distressed calling for safety from land. Both were experiencing the effects of the storm. "Help us, it's too much wind"…"Help us, it's too much water!" Those that were on the ground were trying their best to get off the land. Unbeknownst to them, those that were in the sea were dying to reach the land!

This is the sad reality when one doesn't understand that peace, like India, is a peninsula. Some lost their lives believing that their only option or way of escape was by water. However, those that were in the water knew that that wasn't the case. By now I hope you realize the illustration. Those in the ship represent the 'absence of peace'. Those on land represent the ‚possession of peace'. Everyone experiences adverse situations in life. Someone without peace is hoping and reaching for it. While those that possess it without understanding feel their only option is to relinquish it because of the circumstances surrounding them. We must learn how to live on the Peninsula of Peace.

Let us further our understanding. A 'peninsula' and an 'island' are not the same! An island is an isolated piece of land surrounded by water on every side. Whereas, a peninsula is a piece of land surrounded by water on only three sides. An island is connected to nothing. Normally, a peninsula is an extension of a greater size land. India is the largest peninsula in the world; however, the right storm would make those living there feel like it's an island. The Indian peninsula is actually attached to Asia, which is the largest continent in the world (get it?). Florida is a much smaller peninsula than India. Nevertheless, if pirates decided to attack Florida, they wouldn't just get the Florida Police Department. Consequently, they'd deal with the greatest military in the world... The UNITED STATES of AMERICA!

The point that I'm making is this: We don't have an isolated peace. Our peace is a peninsula. It may be surrounded, but it didn't come from the surroundings! Therefore, the surroundings (trouble, affliction, insurmountable issues, trials, persecution, condemnation, etc.) can't take it away! I'm writing this to assure you...You might feel like an island, but you're really a peninsula.

> *"We don't have an isolated peace. Our peace is a peninsula."*

25

Though you standout surrounded by much, you're connected to a greater! Make sure your peace is connected to Shalom. For what a thing is of will always surface to the capacity of its essence to defend its interest!

5

Spiritual Check-Up

It started at the dining room table as a simple conversation between my wife, daughter, and I over dinner. A comment was made by my wife that I subconsciously took offense to. The evidence of my displeasure was apparent by my response. She told me that "I" was teaching my baby girl bad eating habits by allowing her to eat a couple of cookies a day.

I felt like she was over exaggerating and just spewing out stuff from this new age health kick! I told her that when I was coming up, we used to eat at least a whole pack of cookies each day and we were fine. I carried on with the statement, "kids need sugar for energy because they're active throughout most of the day". She told me,

"That may have been the case THEN, but it doesn't mean that it was right". It was then that I felt like she was challenging my skills as a parent and bringing into question my upbringing. I went off even the more, but this time I took it a little too far. I told her that I don't believe all this junk on TV, its fake, and just a conspiracy.

When I was growing up a salad consisted of lettuce, tomatoes, croutons, a few bacon bits, and dressing. Now it's kale, grass, and stuff that look like leaves off the shade tree. I proceeded to lead a verbal assault on her family members weight (obviously excluding my own), on how I know how to workout (like that had anything to do with the conversation), and how I'm the healthiest person in our household anyway! "So, don't tell me that I'm teaching my baby girl bad eating habits!"

My wife simply refused to continue on with this "healthy debate" and said, "Fine. Your doctor's appointment is next week. I was like, "Okay, let's do it!" I've never had any health challenges in my life. I figured if that's what would give her peace of mind and prove my point to be right, then let's back it up by a medical profession and facts.

We went to the doctor's office as planned, but I must admit my stance was very arrogant. I told the doctor in the beginning, "I'm healthy, as you can see, so let's just get this over with so my point can be proven." She laughed as she proceeded to ask her routine questions.

>**Her:** Mr. Thomas when was the last time you had a check up or physical?
>
>**Me:** About 20 years ago when I played high school sports.
>
>**Her:** Are you allergic to anything?
>
>**Me:** Nope.
>
>**Her:** What is your diet like?
>
>**Me:** Ma'am I eat what I want when I want it.
>
>**Her:** Eat things like what?
>
>**Me:** Everything! I mean my wife tries to feed me grass in a blender, but I told her that's for lizards and not for someone as healthy as myself.

She laughed and proceeded with her questions.

>**Her:** I see that you work out…?
>
>**Me:** I see that you can see very well.
>
>**Her:** Ok Mr. Thomas, we'll just get some urine and blood samples and then you're done for the day. You'll receive a text on your phone with the results in about 2 days. Then we'll go from there to see if there's anything further to address.
>
>**Me:** Cool. Have a wonderful day. Peace out!

This was on a Wednesday. On Friday afternoon I received a text from the doctor's office with my results. I opened the app on my phone only to see what looked like a formula from a Russian Military Chart! Some things were written in black and some items were written in red. To me, "RED" is always an indication of caution. So that sparked a reason for me to have a slight level of concern. Although what I was reviewing was gibberish to me, I had enough sense to assume that the "H's" meant "high" and the "L's" meant "low". Nevertheless, it was the conclusion of the report that shook me. Located in the "comments" section typed in red letters with ALL CAPS was, PLEASE CONTACT YOUR PHYSICIAN IMMEDIATELY TO DISCUSS RESULTS!

I called immediately, but the doctor wouldn't give me any information over the phone no matter how much I tried to persuade her. I spent every bit of 15 minutes trying to convince her that I wouldn't tell a soul if she just let me know what the deal was. She told me that it was against policy to give out personal medical records over the phone and that I must come in to discuss it. I tried everything from bribery to manipulation. From, "Doc, if you tell me now, we can both save gas money" to "Ma'am, I need you to tell me, so I'll know what to pray about!" All to no avail. She found my attempts very comical. She said," Mr. Thomas, you're okay. If it was an emergency, I would've told you." I shot one more shot and missed. Then asked could I come in now, today, Friday?! But the next availability wouldn't be until Monday morning. I had to wait it out, not to mention that Monday was my birthday.

This had to be the longest most torturous weekend of my life! I read every scripture that I knew about healing and prayed every prayer over health. I even asked the Lord, "O God in Your foreknowledge You knew that I would be praying this prayer. So, let the doctor realize that her machine just made a mistake this time!"

Understand, I had never had any health problems in my life, so this really had me tripping. All weekend I was examining myself asking, "Where did this pimple on my forehead come from?" "Is my hair falling out?" "Why am I sneezing? I mean it's cold but it's not that cold!" I was really going through it! Of course, I was at the altar Sunday morning saying, "Lord, please don't let me start the next year of my life off with bad news…"

Finally, Monday morning arrived, and I was the first one at the doctor's office. This time my wife didn't come with me. "Oh how badly I wanted to hold her hand!" Taking a deep sigh, I picked my head up and walked in to hear the news. When the doctor came in, she could see the difference in my face from our first visit. She greeted me and told me that I could have a seat. To me it sounded like, "You might want to sit down for this bad news". With my arms folded I told her, "No, I don't want to have a seat. I'm fine just standing here. So, what's going on with these results?" She laughed and assured me that it wasn't bad so just have a seat.

She began to explain to me that some of my cholesterol levels were higher than normal but not so high I would need medicine or anything. Just more water intake would be a great deal of help for liver enzymes. She then took time to educate me on what healthy eating actually was and how I can identify through the ingredients what's best for me. She asked me what I'd been eating recently and then she laid out a plethora of things to avoid.

She started with "packaged food". I said, "Ma'am, I don't live on a farm. All food comes in a package." I started to name some foods and restaurants that I considered healthy, but her copious "No's" became almost overwhelming. I even mixed in things that I didn't eat but thought were healthy. "Ensure?" No! "Peanut Butter?" No! "Taco Bell?" No! "Chic-fil-la?" No! "Wait a minute…Not even Chic-fil-la? But they're saved! They don't even open on Sundays!" She laughed and said, "Well it depends on what you order from there."

I told her, "Ma'am, I work out and you're telling me all of these things that I shouldn't have." She said, "Mr. Thomas, have you ever heard of 'skinny-fat'?" I said, "Ma'am, probably me and no one else has ever heard of 'skinny-fat'!" I mean it's antithetical like "up-down" or "east-west" or "out-in". "I've never heard of it, what is it?" She said," it's when a person can look good and healthy on the outside but on the inside there's fat that clogs the vital parts. It's deceptive and most don't realize they have it until it's too late. By then the results could be critical and even some grave." I said, "Wow, I can't have that and I'm very grateful for you sharing this with me. But now my question is: How am I supposed to get my protein?" She shook her head and replied, "Mr. Thomas where we live, we don't have a "protein problem". What we do have and suffer from is a NUTRITION PROBLEM!

This statement shook me to the core, and I knew that God was speaking because the revelation began to flow. I became engaged in objective thought. To me, I only associated "protein" with muscles and I honestly only wanted muscles to look nice so that I could "look good". It's not a bad thing. However, nice muscles don't equal good health. I realize that in life, whether personal, church, or humanity we scarcely have a problem with looking good or up to par on the surface but underneath the cosmetics lies what we really know. Furthermore, even deeper beyond our knowledge resides things that can only be made known through investigative demands.

Life's tests must run their course. Examining ourselves is imperative, BUT forensics must take place to reveal the "blood trail". I look forward to us tracing the blood all the way back to Calvary. That way we can identify:

- What the BLOOD has to do with us (relevancy)

- When we've properly used (applied) the BLOOD
- When we've totally disregarded (failed to apply) the BLOOD, but by God's mercy it still spoke for us (in spite of).

6

BLOOD Pressure

It's a health and medical fact that salt raises the blood pressure. Now it's already established that in Jesus Christ we are the "SALT of the Earth". Furthermore, the pressure of the Blood of Jesus is gauged by how WE (salt) apply it. The question is: Have you been operating on the "efficiency" of the Blood or have you been functioning by the "efficacy" of the Blood?

Efficiency vs. Efficacy

EFFICIENCY is the ability to do something well without a waste of time and money. If you want something done quick and effective without the lack of organization - you want efficiency. It's getting the maximum capacity out of the least. An efficiency apartment usually consists of 1 room with everything in it. A bed, a couch, a refrigerator, a table, a TV, a mirror, a sink, a rug, and sometimes a toilet all in 1 room.

Depending on one's assignment, comfortability, tolerance and mobility, an efficiency apartment is "good enough" to get the job done. To each its own. However, not every task is required for the focus to be all in one place! Personal and private matters deserve their own rooms. There are kitchen matters, living room matters, bedroom matters, bathroom matters, and den matters that need to be tended to in their appropriate space. So, while efficiency is "just good enough" -efficacy is "more than enough!" EFFICACY is what I like to call salubrious effectiveness. It's the ability of something to produce the results you want. Let me emphasize: ***Produce the Results You Want!***

The pressure of the BLOOD flowing through our life depends on our mentality, outlook, and application of the BLOOD. If subconsciously you believe that the BLOOD is going to run out or you obtained a good report a time or two by its utilization, so you'll just chill until the next challenge comes… you operate on its efficiency. But I'm here to tell you that **"I"** need it every day! On a good day, bad day, up day, down day, best day or worst day…I gots-to-have-IT because its efficacy is more than enough. The ultimate price was paid by His BLOOD!

*Listen, no matter when or where you're reading at this time,

You have now entered into a prophetic part of this book.

In the beginning MAN forfeited his dominion. God's desire was to reconcile mankind back to Himself, but there was a huge gap because sin separated us! So, our Heavenly Father did a work through sacrificing His Son, Jesus. Now this offering superseded any and every other oblation. It was the ultimate with none greater. It brought/bought mankind back in right standing, opportunity, and relationship with God. It was the supreme sacrifice! Now I want you to take a few moments and pray this prayer:

My Father, My God, By the BLOOD of Your supreme sacrifice on Calvary, Close the Gap in my life-from where I am now to where I need to be!

In Jesus' Mighty Name! Amen!

The efficacy of the Blood exists on a continuum which exceeds any extreme! No matter how intense or severe it gets, rely on the "Efficacy of the Blood"! No matter how things change or shift, rely on the "Efficacy of the Blood"! No matter how chronic or acute the pain; report; or condition may be, you can rely on the "Efficacy of the Blood!" Efficacy is the ability to get the job done satisfactorily. It's one thing to finish a job; it's another

> *"It's one thing to finish a job; it's another thing to finish it WELL."*

thing to finish it well. Some would argue that a mere finish is enough. But you can finish something poorly OR complete a task to your peak performance & capability. However, neither assures that your efforts would conclude to be satisfactory! You gave your ALL:

- ❖ In that relationship…
- ❖ At that job…
- ❖ With those kids…
- ❖ To the career and/or dream…

And it still wasn't enough!

BUT THE BLOOD MAKES THE DIFFERENCE! Because Jesus was the propitiation for our sins!

Propitiation is different from atonement. The 'atonement' was efficient. It satisfied for a moment, until something else happened. Like an apology- then you had to do it again. However, the 'propitiation' gives us peace with God because it pacified His anger and exempts us from His wrath. Isaiah 53:10 says, *"Yet it PLEASED the Lord to bruise Him…"* Luke 12:32 says, *"your Father is PLEASED to give you the kingdom…"* AND BY THAT BLOOD WE ARE AFFORDED TO WALK IN HIS (GOOD) PLEASURE!

7

The Source of Bondage

There are several individual sorts of forensic evidence. Three of the major categories of forensic evidences are: DNA, Fingerprints, and Bloodstain Pattern Analysis (BPA). Through the research provided, one must identify which category the bondage originated from and/or is being driven by.

*DNA- represents the innate parts. This could be ancestral issues passed down from generation to generation. Chains of our forefather's household wickedness, iniquities of our father/mother's house.

*Fingerprints- represent experiences. Things that we have participated in, including witnessed. This in a sense is like biting from the Tree of

39

Knowledge of Good and Evil. You saw what you shouldn't have seen, heard what you shouldn't have heard, and tasted what you shouldn't have put your mouth to.

*Bloodstain Pattern Analysis- represent unprofitable choices fueled by an unhealthy thought process. There are marks of error all over that can be traced back to your bad decision making.

THE FACTS

Here's the process. Forensic scientists first collect samples and preserve the specimen. Afterward, they analyze the scientific data/evidence during the course of investigation. According to many sources, some forensic researchers travel to the scene of the crime in order to collect evidence. Others occupy a lab post, performing analysis on objects brought to them by other individuals.

Since we're dealing in spiritual matters that are beyond the surface, I will be testifying with an expert opinion discovered through the Spirit of God to explain my analysis. As stated in my workbook Warfare Initiative Vol.1, "Natural problems have solutions here and there, but it's not the same for spiritual problems. THEY MUST BE ADDRESSED IN THE SPIRIT REALM!"

MY THESIS

During investigative observation of bondage, one of my

very own thought-provoking theses in the explanation of how bondage comes about is this: "The Butterfly ate the Tree...But why?" Some may resolve their answer with, "because it was hungry". But the way my mind works- I need to go beyond the surface.

MY THEORY

To understand WHY, one must understand the butterfly's life cycle. The life cycle of a butterfly is in 4 stages: egg; larva; pupa; adult.

First, the eggs are laid on the leaf of a tree. Then, 3-7 days later the eggs hatch in the tree and out comes the larva (caterpillar). Once the caterpillar has reached its designed capacity (length & weight) a process takes place in that same tree whereby it wraps itself in a cocoon and metamorphosis occurs. When this process is complete, a butterfly emerges from the tree. This butterfly flies gracefully around now feasting on the nectar of trees.

Here's my question: How is it that the same element that provided refuge, shade, and shelter attracts the butterfly to eat it? It's simple: Because during the caterpillar stage (larva), tree is all the caterpillar ate. Tree is already in the butterfly and it's attracted to what's within itself! (naturally and spiritually...Whoa!) Its 'capacity' enabled its 'capability'. The same capacity that made it possible to reach butterfly (adult) stage of life has come to maturity and has given it the capability to eat what once fed the capacity.

BE-COME

Who you 'are' is who you (will) 'be'. Now, who you choose to 'be' is what you 'become'. Once you 'become' know that ‚Be-is-coming'! The butterfly is full of tree. So, tree (inside) attracts tree (outside). In much the same manner, you attract who you are being not just who you are doing! We are human-beings not human-doings!

Psalm 18:26 says, "To the pure You show Yourself pure…" God is not going tit-for-tat; you do this, and I'll do that! No. If that was the case, He would've killed David and allowed all his wives to get raped (based on what David did to Uriah). David was a man after God's own heart. 'After' means David possessed it. Listen, He POSSESSED the very HEART of GOD! 'Own' expresses the same preciousness as 'My Only Begotten' (John 3:16). David was not chasing God's heart; David had the essence and interest of God's own heart! So, "to the pure (God) will show (Himself) pure" doesn't mean if you 'do pure' God will "match you" with purity. No, it means to those who are pure/have become pure; the purity of who you are will attract the purity of who God is.

> *"Who you choose to 'be' is what you 'be-come'."*

On the flip side, if you find yourself overwhelmed by a

bondage it's because either you're a bondage yourself, you're a bondage to someone else, and/or there's a bondage within that identifies with the external

8

Forensic Proofs

FORENSIC PROOF #1 (The Pharaoh in You)

There were NO ‚works of the flesh' mentioned in the Old Testament that were evident like in the New Testament (Galatians 5:19-21). However, we do find that there were attributes of evil, rebellion, wicked kings, pharaoh, etc. The Lord showed me that the only way one will stop attracting bondage or get out of bondage is to get the bondage out of them. This requires for you to deal with "THE PHARAOH IN YOU"! Come on, don't deny it! The evidence shows that your own conscious caught you on camera!

"Why do you look at the speck of sawdust in your brother's eye and pay no attention to the plank (log/beam) in your own eye?

How can you say to your brother, 'Let me take the speck out of your own eye', when all the time there's a plank (log/beam) in your own eye? You hypocrites, first take the plank (log/beam) out of your own eye, and then you will see clearly to remove the speck from your brother's eye..."
Matthew 7:3-5 (NIV)

The harsh reality of this passage is that the reason you can easily identify the speck is because the speck very well may be a piece of your log! One cannot see around a log in their eye. All they can do is identify with the log and pieces of log (speck of sawdust) that are around. So, bondage attracts bondage because bondage can easily identify (a lesser) bondage. The reason your life may be attracting a Pharaoh in your workplace (boss), Pharaoh in your relationships, Pharaoh in your finances, etc. is because those external pharaohs are attracted to "The Pharaoh in You"!

SPOTTING PHARAOH

During Moses' time, Pharaoh was the main antagonist to the Children of Israel (Exodus Ch. 1:8-14:28). Pharaoh was a king, a ruler in ancient Egypt. A RULER has 3 interpretations of use:

> 1) One that rules
> 2) Instrument of measurement
> 3) Explicit regulations

Pharaoh enforces dominion by operating in all three. The Pharaoh in You: 1) endorses one to situationally exercise ultimate power or authority over others (whether legal or illegal); 2) to size another up by judgement of your own standards versus what that person actually stands for themselves; 3) to impose unknown and/or unrealistic expectations on another based on your own gratifications.

Although geographically Egypt is a country in northeastern Africa, spiritually Egypt represents hard bondage. Pharaoh was one that:

- Made it hard on others by way of dictatorship
- Did not worship the One True God
- Became renown for refusing to release the Children of Israel

God sent Moses to tell him, "Let My people GO"! So, it must be addressed before TRUE deliverance can take place in your life. You will sense the "deliverance anointing" as I ask these questions:

- ❖ What are you holding on to that the Lord is saying "Let Go!"?
- ❖ Why are you holding on to it?
- ❖ Who are you not releasing in prayer?
- ❖ What have you not relinquished control over?
- ❖ What are you holding over somebody else's head?

❖ What areas have you NOT yielded to God for His glory the way that He wants to be glorified?

Whew! Answering those questions sincerely, is a 'deliverance session' all by itself! The realization that what you're holding on to is keeping <u>you</u> from being set free brings liberation. However, if you're comfortable with harboring the weight, the sad reality is you have accepted your own Egypt!

FORENSIC PROOF #2 (Self Inflicted Cages)

As mentioned early on, there is a unique difference between a trap and a snare. When someone or something is trapped, it knows or has a clear sense of it right away. The reaction is normally that of imminent danger (spontaneous panic). With a snare, one doesn't realize that they're trapped until they try to get out. The snare could be in operation for years before they reach the realization (delayed panic). Just because there's freedom of speech in the natural doesn't mean it's so in the spiritual, emotional, mental, etc. There are particular bondages that Satan and haters aren't responsible for, and these are what I call "self-inflicted cages".

Above all bondages, self-inflicted cages are the most common. Why? Because they're determined by how vocal, confident, and analytical you are. You can unintentionally set over 1000 of these cages a day in your life so being mindful and disciplined is key.

How To Avoid Self-Inflicted Cages:

#STOP talking so much!

> *"When words are many, transgression is not lacking, but whoever restrains his lips is prudent"*
> *Proverbs 10:19 (ESV)*

Your own words are yoking you. A lot of what you speak against has nothing to do with you, but you still put your mouth on it. Now whatever 'it' may be varies (person, place, policy, etc.) Here's the question to ask yourself: how has ‚it' directly affected YOU? You cannot connect it with your emotions. God can use anything in creation to move your life forward. However, you cancel yourself from the grace of your unknown future by murmuring now.

#STOP using yourself as an example!

Statements like "if it was me" or "say for instance" are unnecessary proposals. Don't put it on you if it's not you or for you! Refrain your mouth from giving you vivid convictions. The truth is that "your own mouth can deceive your heart" and as a man thinketh in his heart, so is he (Proverbs 23:7). Hear wisdom speak: Your "say for instance" is "saying for existence"!

#STOP comparing yourself/life (to the negative)

Things were going fine in your reality until you started watching reality TV shows! Now the pressure is applied to everyone around you to fulfill an image. Listen, once the camera starts, it's no longer a reality. Plus, they give Image Awards to actors. Besides, comparison is a contentment killer. Peace lost is a byproduct to consistent contrasting. The rich have their own issues as well as the poor. The way of the wealthy is mastery of their own lane.

#STOP gossiping

Being messy breeds mess in your own life. It's the poison to a pure heart. We must hold ourselves accountable in this area by consciously refusing to partake. Do what works for you. Something that I found therapeutic was to match the gossip with 2x as much prayer for the person/situation. So, if the conversation lasts an hour, pray for 2 hours. Before long you'll learn the effect of prioritizing your prayer sectors.

#STOP being so judgmental!

That's a spirit! There's a difference between critical thinking and just being critical. When you're a critical thinker, you take time and effort to evaluate an issue in order to formulate a judgement. When you're only thinking critically, you form a judgement on a subject matter regardless of if there's an issue or not. This normally expresses criticism that's not constructive. All criticism is not bad, but too much of anything is not good and could be an indication that your efforts are driven by a spirit (i.e. critical spirit).

#STOP the pinning blame!

It has been said that "expectation is the breeding ground to miracles". On the other side of the spectrum, "negative anticipation could lead to debacle". When you have a preconceived liability against another, it becomes an ungodly bias. The fact is that indirectly you're expecting something to go wrong! So if/when they do go wrong, you've already locked in your heart "who" to point the finger at. When in all actuality, it's just the fruition of your suspense.

For example, say you played a major part in not allowing "such-and-such" in your child's life. Now at every success of that child, you graciously accept all the praise. However, every hiccup or failure from that child you say, "it's because such-and-such wasn't there". Partly, that very well may be true, but you don't accept your part (participation) in that truth. Pinning blame keeps accusations in the balance. It's a self-righteous excuse to hold things against another. This exempts you from flowing in a spirit of excellence because apart from your part, you're anticipating holding someone else accountable.

FORENSIC PROOF #3 (You Haven't Decided that Enough is Enough)

Every human being will be defined by what they're sure about! Somethings have not stopped in your life simply because you've never told those things to stop! There's a reserved compromise in the recesses of your mind that keeps you unsure if you really want to end the occurrence. The same holds true with starting something new.

> "...a doubleminded man is UNSTABLE in all his ways..."
> James 1:8 (KJV)

> "purify your hearts ye doubleminded..."
> James 4:8 (KJV)

Doublemindedness is a condition of the heart. It causes you to never take "a thing by the throat" due to neglected absoluteness. This is ever so true in the ministry of deliverance. When you truly CARE, you can't care how it comes off! Passiveness can cause casualty.

There was a great pioneer of the faith, a Man of God, who shared an extraordinary instance of a time he had to address witches. A decision was made to host the largest Witch Convention in his city. This would bring in over 15,000

> "When you truly CARE, you can't care how it comes off!"

witches across the world. To him, this was an insult. He took it personally and said, "It's not happening"! The word got back to the witches' chief administrator of the convention and he released a verbal assault against the Man of God via media saying, "Not even God Himself can stop this convention from happening". Reports of that, what seemed to be a strong comment, were relayed to the Man of God to see what he thought about it. The Man of God replied, "He's right! God doesn't have to come down and stop it. I'm here!" Needless to say, it didn't happen! Not only that, but from that one stance of being determined with a made-up mind, his nation is the ONLY nation in the world that has implemented in their constitution: "NO WITCHCRAFT IS ALLOWED TO BE PRACTICED IN THIS COUNTRY" (paraphrased).

Quit being so careful about what you know needs to be eradicated. People who take care don't take charge and people who take charge usually don't take care!

Philippians 4:6 says: "Be careful for nothing..." (KJV)

One of my mottos is: "Anything worth being careful about is worth being prayerful about!"

MAKE UP YOUR MIND

When you decide to cool your house, the air conditioning thermostat is set to a particular temperature. However, the house doesn't immediately become that temperature. Nevertheless, the thermostat is "set", and you know that temperature is coming because your whole air conditioning unit (inside and outside) is working to reach that goal. Could it be that things are persisting in your life because you haven't had the right mind-SET? A life in limbo is a losing life. You're in bondage of waiting to see how things turn out instead of DECREEING and DECLARING!

Advisory Notice: "The enemy is waiting to see how things turn out! Why are you just gonna wait with him?" Do something! Make a choice. Deuteronomy 30:19 says,

"I call heaven and earth to record this day against you, that I have set before you life and death, blessing and cursing, therefore CHOOSE life, that both thou and thy seed may live:"
(KJV)

I realize that God did not make winners and losers. He made CHOOSERS! The best choice to make when it comes to making a decision is the right choice. The worst thing you can do when it comes to making a decision is NOT to make a choice at all, forget the bad choice. Within every decision of not making a choice, a choice is being decided for you.

"God did not make winners and losers. He made CHOOSERS!"

CHOOSE What Is Salubriously Conducive

I live in Houston, Texas. Now, I can get in my truck and drive 10 1/2hrs north to reach a city called Paris, Texas, OR I can jump on a plane and fly 10 1/2hrs to arrive in Paris, London! It's my choice to go further with the time I'm given. Furthermore, I REFUSE TO SPEND ALL THAT TIME JUST TO STAY IN THE SAME STATE! (state of mind, financial state, state of relationship, state of status, state of etc.) Come on! Choose to refuse!

FORENSIC PROOF #4 (Unregulated Fear)

It's been stated that the phrase "Do not fear" and those of the like appear exactly 365 times in the Bible. Personally, I've never counted. Nevertheless, I get it and think it's pretty cool when paralleled to the 365 days in a year. I don't believe however that we need a daily emphasis on what NOT to do, but rather we need emphasis on what we SHOULD do. My opinion doesn't negate the fact that the devil seeks to terrorize us constantly. Therefore, a reminder from God to live everyday fearlessly is empowering.

It's widely propagated and taught that faith is the opposite of fear. In my estimation, I see that not to be true. I do sincerely believe at times that it's not faith you really need, but rather COURAGE. Fear is not the absence of faith, and faith is not the absence of fear. Fear is a territory that faith either dominates or is dominated by. That's why to Joshua (Joshua 1:9) God didn't say, "Be of good faith". No. Instead He tells him, "Be strong and of good courage!" Courage is not the absence of fear, but courage is the audacity in the presence of fear. Fear is a reaction; courage is a decision.

Now the Bible has a harsh reality to those who lives are dominated by fear. Revelation 21:7-8:

"He that overcometh shall inherit all things; and I will be his God, and he shall be My son.[7] But the FEARFUL, and unbelieving, and the abominable, and murderers, and whoremongers, and sorcerers, and idolaters, and all liars, shall have their part in the lake which burneth with fire and brimstone: which is the second death.[8]" (KJV)

The interesting thing about this scripture is that "the FEARFUL" is first on the list. In theory with The Law of First Mention, what's listed first is of most importance because everything else is either filtered through it or fueled by it. Take a look:

* FEARFUL; unbelieving; abominable; whoremongers; sorcerers; idolaters; liars

Now one may say "I could never be a whoremonger or a murderer!" or "I hate idolaters and liars!", but yet be fearful and unbelieving. The whoremonger could say, "well at least I'm not fearful" and be justified in that statement yet guilty of the rest. The fact is, no matter how commonplace being fearful has become to you, despite the relativity, it's still on the same level with the rest.

THERE IS A REMEDY, Fear Not!

"There is NO FEAR in LOVE; but perfect love casteth out fear: because fear hath torment. He that feareth is not MADE PERFECT in LOVE."
1 John 4:18 (KJV)

You see, there is no fear in love; not in faith! Love "castETH": continually casts out fear, not just once! "ETH" is an ad infinitum meaning "without end or limit". Again, NOT JUST ONCE. Why? Because fear hath torment. Torment is the absence of mercy. There is no gentleness without mercy, and gentleness is LOVE's conduct! "He that feareth is not made perfect in love…" Do you see it? The areas of your life that you find fear may expose to you an insecurity, insufficiency, lack, inadequacy, etc. Understand this: that's not who you are! When you call yourself those things and allow others to feed that deficiency, it binds you into believing that is your identity. When actually the truth is: any area of your life that you find fear is an indication that LOVE hasn't been PERFECTED in that area. So, it's not a

"Gentleness is love's conduct."

condemnation thing. It's more of an awareness. When you notice it, simply pray: "Lord perfect Your love in this area of my life."

For those thoughts you get when he/she goes somewhere - Lord perfect Your love

For when you doubt you'll get the job or promotion-Lord perfect Your love

Stepping out to do what you haven't done before- Lord perfect Your love

"Perfect Love" is "Perfecting Love"! Allow that perfecting love and its power to govern your life into all liberation. AMEN.

FORENSIC PROOF #5 (Perpetuated Past)

Jesus gave a marksman reference about dealing with the past: **Remember Lot's Wife** (Luke 17:32). For some of us, we know that it is only by God's mercy that we escaped our past. This is the same for Abraham's nephew Lot and his family. God was about to destroy Sodom and Gomorrah and granted them the mercy to leave. In that same mercy, He gave them strict instructions not to look back. Consumed with the things of the city, Lot's wife looked back and was instantly turned into a pillar of salt. In a glance, she became "symbolic seasoning" for the past. When you're looking back, you're no good for what's ahead. Some of us can't move forward in life because we're looking backwards.

"Remember ye not the former things, Neither the things of old. Behold, I will do a new thing…"
Isaiah 43:18-19 (KJV)

Sometimes you can't see the "new thing" because you're constantly considering the "old thing". You miss the good in a new thing because of what you consider good in the old thing!

"Therefore if any man be in Christ, he is a NEW CREATURE: old things are passed away; behold, all things have become new."
2 Corinthians 5:17 (KJV)

New creature- Not the same

Old things are passed- Your past has passed! Seriously, you need to make an obituary of who you were. Write a eulogy and preach the funeral to your "old man". Some of us have not officially allowed the past to be cremated. NOT BURIED- because you'll exhume it!

Behold- Look! Not glance. When driving, you look out of the windshield but only glance at the rearview and side mirrors for safety.

All things are become new *MAJOR REVELATION*: Anything NEW doesn't have a past! If you catch this in your inner most being, deliverance can take place right where you are!

A NEW THING DOESN'T HAVE A PAST

Now that we've established that, what do we call the happenings before we became a new creature? Though a new thing doesn't have a past, there is an era before 'new'. It's called HISTORY. If you go to a Bentley Motors (which by the way, the cars are never on sale) you won't see a sales representative arguing with the service department over a screw dropped while putting the car together. The assembly process has nothing to do with the new product in their presence. So, a car with zero mileage still has history even though it hasn't been driven. The only history that a new thing has is being made! All of the pain, pleasure, pits, and platforms had its time and purpose. Don't put yourself in bondage by being caught up on what made you who you are today!

> *"Your past has passed."*

From "Raw Material" To "Luxury, that's never on sale"!

From "Trash" To "Kingdom"!

From "Works of Darkness" To "His Marvelous Light"!

Listen, the past of light is not darkness. The past of light is being translated. Don't focus on who/what you were, instead, concentrate on the translation power that brought you to who you are now.

FORENSIC PROOF #6 (Mental Imagery)

There is a nation where you can be anything you want to be and have anything you want to have. It's highly promoted in the prophetic and can provoke manifestations of plenty sorts. I advise everyone to at least set aside some time to visit every day. That place is "image-nation" i.e. your imagination.

The bondage of "Mental Imagery" is negative imaginations depicted in our soul. If not taken captive, they will torment you without mercy. Mark Twain once spoke on worry this way. "I've suffered a great many catastrophes in my life and most of them never happened". This means he experienced the effects and stress of an outcome that never came to pass. The bondage of Mental Imagery is not always the individual's fault. In fact, there are two aspects that lend negativity the law of residency. I find access to either be "Involuntary" or "Incited".

"Involuntary Imagery" means something happened out of your control. It was traumatic, and you saw what you weren't trying to see. Now you can't get the thought of it out of your mind. For example: Some people can no longer drive due to physical injury from a bad accident. Some others don't drive because of mental injury from an accident. They're physically capable, but just can't seem to get that image of the moment out of their mind.

I remember coming home early one day and allowing our babysitter to leave ahead of her usual time. Normally, while my son would be with the sitter, my daughter would grab a snack and stay in my room until I get home. This day in particular, I had an unction to go home earlier than planned. Once I got home, sure enough my daughter was in my bedroom alone laying down. As soon as I came in the room, a spirit of sleepiness hit me. So, I grabbed my son, released the sitter, and laid in the bed with my daughter. Moments later, my daughter crawled on the opposite side of me, (which I never permit because I don't want her to fall out of the bed) told me her leg hurt and went to sleep right there on me. I was very sleepy at the time, so I was in-and-out of consciousness because my son was still awake.

All of a sudden, I felt something warm on my leg. When I looked over my daughter's shoulder, her face was down in the mattress. She was twitching and having a seizure. I had never experienced this in my life. She seized for every bit of 15 minutes. I immediately grabbed her and my son, ran downstairs and across the street to a neighbor for help. By the time I got to the neighbor's house she was already blue in the face. The thought came to my mind, "You've prayed for others and even raised babies up from near death, BUT you can't even help your own." Of course, that was the enemy, but I remember looking to heaven saying, "Lord, in my arms? You can't let this happen in my hands".

To make a long story short, we went to the fire station, took an ambulance to the emergency room, she regained consciousness and to God be the Glory we overcame the attack with victorious health! Afterwards, it was 3 weeks before I slept in my bed again and another month before I even went on that particular SIDE of the bed where the accident occurred. For days in and days out I cried because I couldn't get that image of her, blue faced, out of my mind. The "what ifs" still knock me to my knees. Out of all that I've seen and been through in life, that by far was the worst experience in the least amount of time. To overcome the torment associated with that "involuntary imagery" I began to consider more of the "little miracles" that had to take place in order for her to survive. Thank God!

"Incited Imagery" is when one volunteers to encourage the visuals of disturbance. This is by your own volition, where you choose to imagine the worst. You stir it up, provoke it, fuel it, and then allow it to play out in your mind. The bondage is rightfully there because "as a man thinketh in his heart, so is he" (Proverbs 23:7). So, you began to act out externally what you perceived to be real internally. This is usually manifested in a bad attitude, isolation, suspicion, interrogation, etc.

FORENSIC PROOF #7 (Contaminated Spirit)

There's a saying that goes, "What you miss in the wash; hope to catch in the rinse". I find this statement to hold a heavy dose of truth with spiritual implications. As much as we rely on the finished work of Christ, it's not amiss to question why the power isn't working in us the way it was promised to work. I don't believe that God is the problem, neither is He reluctant to work that good work in us. There's a clog somewhere as to why some things come out of us surprisingly and why we don't see deliverance from within like we ought. It's because we don't realize that some things are connected to our cleansing! Some of us operate from: "a Contaminated Spirit"! WAIT! WHAT?! NOT POSSIBLE! YES!!!

How is this Possible?

You see, we're taught that MAN is a spirit, that lives in a body, and possesses a soul. This is very true. Furthermore, we're also taught that once we accept Jesus as our personal Lord and Savior, the Holy Spirit comes and lives in our spirit. This is also true. However, from that point on it's insinuated that the spirit man is set and all the issues in life can only come from either externally, the flesh, or the battle in the soul. But I ran across a passage of scripture that shook me to the core:

"Since we have these promises, dear friends, we need to

cleanse ourselves from everything that contaminates BODY and SPIRIT and live a holy life in the fear of God"
2 Corinthians 7:1 (GW)

"cleanse"..."body and spirit"...

"Body" in this context is not speaking of the fleshly nature but rather of our physical body and human nature. Now "spirit" I know is often used interchangeably with "soul", but I found it not to be so in this context. I looked up "soul" here in the Greek and got the word "psyche" which means "breath", "spirit" (greek.5590). However, in this particular scripture the word "spirit" gave me "pneumatos" which in Greek means "WIND, breath, spirit" (greek.4151). Now there's a separation between soul and spirit. This Scripture tells me something contrary to popular belief which will cause many to re-evaluate their stance on the operation of the tri-partite being of man. This scripture didn't mention the "soul". So, it's possible to have a "body-spirit connection" bypassing the "soul". I know many will disagree, but how? This is the same phenomenon that takes place when it comes to speaking in tongues (1 Corinthians 14:14). But we're taught to exclude the spirit and just work on the soul. That's where we miss true deliverance!

Head vs. Heart

When it comes to faith, the Bible speaks a lot about

believing in your 'heart'. Sadly, a lot of people only truly believe in their 'head'. It's hard to tell until a test of faith arises. The head is connected to the soulish part of us: mind, will, emotions, etc. The heart is much deeper and carries a divine connection. The heart is the place where the soul and spirit meet. It's a meeting place!

When men met with God in the Bible, they built an altar. In much the like, the heart of man is the Altar of man! Now this is very personal. This is the meeting place with exclusive access. This revelation is why "once saved always saved" is a lie. Because we use scriptures like "no man can pluck me out of His hand" and phrases like, "not a devil in hell can do anything to me". I agree but understand, this meeting place is too sacred and personal for a man to pluck or a demon to do. The only person that can reach this altar is YOU! So yes, it's very true that no one can take your salvation, BUT YOU very well can forfeit it! No man can pluck you out of His hand BUT YOU can jump overboard yourself. Whatever you "announce" can be "renounced". THIS is a thing between you and God only.

> *"The heart is the place where the soul and spirit meet."*

Though the God within you cannot dwell with sin, what He's shown me was how powerful our spirit really is and its jurisdiction. It's not that we bring filth inside the spirit. Rather, we bring it within the vicinity of our spirit.

So Yes, Holy Spirit is still there, but there's an influence at the heart (altar) that causes us not to exercise God's option at times. Guard your heart, for it is the vicinity of the spirit.

9

Our Victory

We have a redeemed right to be free; it's our inheritance! The Blood of Jesus has made this possible for us. From Gethsemane to Golgotha, Jesus shed His Blood seven times. Seven is the number of completion. His Blood is sufficient for any thing, any day, and will supersede every power. Apply this to your being as often as necessary.

7 Times Jesus Shed His Blood

- Sweat (Luke 22:44) "The condition of hematidrosis" = overcoming the flesh
- Bruise (Isaiah 53:5) "Iniquities" = generational curses
- 39 Stripes (Isaiah 53:5) "39 root causes to every sickness & disease that exists" = healing

- Crown of Thorns (John 19:2) "Mocking/Undermining His Lordship" = sanctified mind
- Hands (Deut. 15:10/Psalm 90:17 "connections and relationship" = everything you touch shall prosper
- Feet (Joshua 1:3) "destiny" = wherever your feet tread or the sole of your feet touch, you have dominion
- Piercing of the Side (Psalm 69:20) "blood and water" = His heart was broken so yours and mine don't have to be!

PROPHETIC APPLICATION

You will not find in the Bible the phrase "I plead the Blood". Nevertheless, I understand it because the Bible is a legal document. This phrase came about in the early 1900's with the Pentecostal movement. It holds much relevancy to spiritual warfare and setting a parameter. Furthermore, defense STOPS, but OFFENSE scores! Pleading the Blood of Jesus is a defensive strategy. Defense covers but offense conquers. To score on the offensive side of the Blood you begin to "Proclaim the Victory of the Blood". When you proclaim the victory of the Blood, you position yourself for victory every time. When sickness, terror, or death is coming against us, we PLEAD the Blood for covering and Passover. But to see the power of the Spirit and the dead come back to life- we proclaim the victory of the Blood which is everlasting freedom!

The Initial Step to Freedom

Heavenly Father,
I come to you, just as I am, a sinner in need of salvation. I confess with my mouth and believe in my heart that Jesus Christ is my personal Lord and Savior. I believe that You raised Jesus from the dead in order to save me. Right now, I receive Jesus into my heart to reign in my life. I thank You Lord for saving me right now. Holy Spirit I invite you into my heart. Help me to live a truly Christian life and empower me to make decisions that honor God. From today, I serve you with all of me.
Thank You for making me a Child of God.
In Jesus' Name, Amen.

About the Author

Karey Thomas is a dynamic Evangelist, entrepreneur, life coach, strategist, and thought leader of this generation. He Pastors Ambition of Christ Restoration Center in Houston, TX and ignites change in lives across the world through his Inspire By Fire NonProfit Organization and KT Empowers coaching program. His passion is to see lives transformed through targeted, impactful teaching and the empowerment to fulfill their God-given purpose.

For more information and booking opportunities, please visit: www.ktempowers.com